The Religion Of The Indians Of California

A. L. Kroeber

Printing Statement:

Due to the very old age and scarcity of this book, many of the pages may be hard to read due to the blurring of the original text, possible missing pages, missing text, dark backgrounds and other issues beyond our control.

Because this is such an important and rare work, we believe it is best to reproduce this book regardless of its original condition.

Thank you for your understanding.

THE RELIGION OF THE INDIANS OF CALIFORNIA

BY

A. L. KROEBER.

Fundamentally the religion of the Indians of California was very similar to that of savage and uncivilized races the world over. Like all such peoples, the California Indians were in an animistic state of mind, in which they attributed life, intelligence, and especially supernatural power, to virtually all living and lifeless things. They lacked no less the ideas and practices of shamanism, the universal accompaniment of animism: namely, the belief that certain men, through communication with the animate supernatural world, had the power to accomplish what was contrary to, or rather above, the events of daily ordinary experience, which latter in so far as they were distinguished from the happenings caused by supernatural agencies, were of natural, meaningless, and, as it were, accidental origin. As in most parts of the world, belief in shamanistic power was centered most strongly about disease and death, which among most tribes were not only believed to be dispellable but to be entirely caused by shamans. In common with the other American Indians, those of California made dancing, and with it always singing, a conspicuous part of nearly all their ceremonies that were of a public or tribal nature. They differed from almost all other tribes of North America in showing a much weaker development of the ritualism, and symbolism shading into pictography, that constitute perhaps the most distinctive feature of the religion of the Americans as a whole. Practically all the approaches to a system

---

* This paper may be cited as Univ. Calif. Publ. Am. Arch. Ethn., Vol. 4, No. 6.

of writing devised in North America, whether in Mexico, Yucatan, or among the tribes of the United States and Canada, are the direct outcome of a desire of religious expression. The California Indians however were remarkably free from even traces of this tendency, equally in their religion and in the more practical aspects of their life. In many parts of North America, and more often where the culture was considerably developed than where it was rude, there was a considerable amount of fetishism, not of the crass and so to speak superstitious type of Africa, but rather as an accompaniment and result of over-symbolism. This fetishistic tendency was very slightly developed in California, and this in spite of—or as an Americanist could more properly say on account of—the generally rude and primitive condition of culture. By contrast, as the action and the visible symbol were a less important means of religious expression, the word, both spoken and sung, was of greater significance in California. The weakness of the ritualistic tendency is however again marked in the circumstance that the exact form of religious speech was frequently less regarded than its substance. In this aspect the Indians of California differed widely from such nations as the Egyptians and the peoples of Asia, where the efficacy of the word and speech used for a religious purpose was usually directly dependent upon the accuracy of their external and audible rendering, even to their pronunciation and intonation.

As an ethnographic province the greater part of California plainly forms a unit. There are, however, two portions of the present political state that showed much cultural distinctness in times of native life and that must usually be kept apart in all matters of ethnological and religious consideration. One of these divergent culture areas comprised the extreme northwestern corner of the state, in the drainage of the lower Klamath and about Humboldt Bay. The other consisted of what is now usually known as Southern California, extending from the Tehachapi pass and mountains in the interior, and from Point Conception on the coast, southward to the Mexican boundary. The religion of the Indians of the peninsula of Lower California is very little known from literature, and the people themselves are almost extinct. It is probable that it was more or less different from the forms of religion occurring in Southern California, that is to say, the southern part of the American state of California. Ethnographically Southern California was considerably diversified. The tribes of the plains and mountains near the sea must be distinguished on the one hand from those of the desert interior and of the valley of the Colorado river, and on the other from those of the Santa Barbara archipelago and the adjacent coast of the mainland to the north. The latter island group of tribes has become entirely extinct without leaving more than the merest trace of records of its religion. The two other groups, the seaward and the interior, apparently presented a much greater uniformity in religion than in their material and social life, so much so that in the present connection all the tribes of Southern California of whom anything is known may be regarded as constituting a single ethnographic province. The culture of the small Northwestern area was in every way, and that of the larger Southern province at least in some respects, more highly organized and complex than that of the still larger and principal Central region, which comprised at least two-thirds of the state and which, if such a selection is to be made, must be considered as the most typically Californian.

The religious practices of the Indians of California fall into three well marked divisions: (1) such observances as are followed and executed by individuals, although their perpetuation is traditionary and tribal; that is to say, customary observances; (2) individual practices resting upon a direct personal communication of an individual with the supernatural world; in other words, shamanism; (3) observances and practices which are not only the common property of the tribe by tradition, but in which the entire tribe or community directly or indirectly participates; in other words, ceremonies.

CUSTOMARY OBSERVANCES BY INDIVIDUALS.

Customary observances are as strongly developed as farther north along the Pacific slope. This entire western coast region thus forms a unit that differs from the interior and eastern parts of the continent, in which such observances are usually a less conspicuous feature than public and tribal ceremonies. By far the most important of the customary observances in California are those relating to death. Next come those connected with birth and sexual functions. Beliefs and practices centering about the individual's name are of importance particularly in so far as they are connected with the customs relating to death. There are restrictions and superstitions as to food, but these are not more numerous than seems generally to have been the case among the North American Indians, and certainly of much less importance than in the Pacific island world and Australia.

Death was considered to cause defilement and almost everywhere brought after it purification ceremonies. In the Northwestern region these were particularly important, and among such tribes as the Hupa and Yurok the observance of religious purification from contact with the dead, the most essential part of which was the recitation of a certain formula, was the most stringently exacted religious custom. The method of disposing of the dead varied locally between burial and cremation, cremation being practiced over at least half of the state. Air burial and sea burial were nowhere found. Mourning, which consisted primarily of singing and wailing, began immediately upon death and continued for about a day, sometimes longer by the immediate relatives of the deceased. Among some tribes this mourning commenced with full vigor some time before impending death, often during the full consciousness of the patient and with his approval. Mutilations on the part of the mourners were not practiced to any great degree, except that the hair was almost universally cut more or less, especially by the women. Among many tribes the widow, but she only, cut or burned off all her hair. Mourning observances were almost always carried further by the women than men. Among some tribes of the Sierra Nevada the widow did not speak from the time of her husband's death until the following annual tribal mourning ceremony, except to one attendant, or, in cases of actual necessity, to women only. In the Sierra Nevada was found also the custom of the widow smearing her face and breast with pitch, which was not washed or removed until this annual ceremony. Except in the case of the Northwestern tribes, who possessed more elaborately constructed houses of wood, the house in which a death had occurred was not used again, but was burned. Objects that had been in personal contact or associated with the deceased were similarly shunned and destroyed. The name of the dead was not spoken. Even the word which constituted his name was not used in ordinary discourse, a circumlocution or newly coined word being employed. It is certain that this stringently observed custom has been a factor in the marked dialectic differentiation of the languages of California. The mention of the name of the dead, whether intentionally or accidentally, in some cases aroused feelings of fear connected with his spirit, but more generally was objected to as causing grief, which appears to have been actually and often intensely felt on such occasions. In Northwestern California the naming of the dead could be compensated for only by the payment of a considerable sum. Practically the only form of curse or malediction known, other than an occasional indirect allusion to the object of the malediction as being in the condition of a corpse, was a reference to his dead relatives. Some property, but more rarely food, was buried with the dead. The idea that such articles were for his use in the world of the dead was not so strong a motive for such acts as, on the one hand, the feeling that the objects had been defiled by association with him, and on the other, the desire to give expression to the sincerity of the mourning by the destruction of valuables. On the whole, however, the immediate observances of death paled in importance before the annual communal mourning ceremony, which was everywhere, except in the Northwestern region, one of the most deeply rooted and spectacular acts of worship.

Observances connected with sexual functions, including birth, are next in importance after those relating to death. The menstruating woman was everywhere regarded as unclean, and excluded especially from acts of worship. Not infrequent was the conception that she contaminated food, especially meat; in other words those varieties of food which were at once more highly prized and at the same time, through being obtained with less regularity and only through special and skilled exertions, regarded as most directly under the control and influence of supernatural powers. Among many tribes, as elsewhere in America and other continents, she was excluded from the living-house as well as from the ceremonial chamber, and confined to the menstrual hut. As elsewhere in North America, the custom in this regard however varied from tribe to tribe, the menstrual hut not having been used in some localities even in purely aboriginal times. Not only was seclusion, as a means of preventing contact and association, frequently required of the woman for the protection of others, but her refraining from all but the most necessary activity was sometimes deemed essential for her own good.

All these observances were greatly intensified at the time of a girl's first menstruation, a condition for which most of the languages of California possess a distinctive and often unanalyzed word. The girl at this period was thought to be possessed of a particular degree of supernatural power, and this was not always regarded as entirely defiling or malevolent. Often, however, there was a strong feeling of the power of evil inherent in her condition. Not only was she secluded from her family and the community, but an attempt was made to seclude the world from her. One of the injunctions most strongly laid upon her was not to look about her. She kept her head bowed and was forbidden to see the world and the sun. Some tribes covered her with a blanket. Many of the customs in this connection resembled those of the North Pacific Coast most strongly, such as the prohibition to the girl to touch or scratch her head with her hand, a special implement being furnished her for the purpose. Sometimes she could eat only when fed and in other cases fasted altogether. Some form of public ceremony, often accompanied by a dance and sometimes by a form of ordeal for the girl, was practiced nearly everywhere. Such ceremonies were well developed in Southern California, where a number of actions symbolical of the girl's maturity and subsequent life were performed. Certain tribes, however, including at least one in the Northwestern area and certain of those in the Sierra region, did not practice public ceremonies of this type.

Religious customs connected with birth consisted in part of observances before the birth of the child, in part of observances relating to it after birth, and especially of restrictions imposed on one or both of its parents after birth. Practices affecting the child itself, or the mother before its birth, related in great part to food. In the Northwest the newly born child was fed for a number of days only on a soup of vegetable substance resembling milk. The newly born child was washed, often repeatedly, among many tribes. The mother after a birth was regarded as more or less defiled, though this feeling usually did not approach in intensity those connected with either death or the woman's periodical functions. Either the mother or both father and mother were usually enjoined from activity for some time after a birth, the motive being not only protection of the child but of themselves. This idea is especially developed among the Yokuts of the southern San Joaquin valley. The couvade in its strict form, with restrictions and observances which are imposed entirely upon the father to the exclusion of the mother, does not seem to be found.

Observances regulating or restricting the use of food were in the main connected with the customs relating to death, sexual functions, and birth. That is to say it was primarily the persons affected by these occurrences, and next to these such as were engaged in acts of intense worship or shamanistic practices, who were prohibited from using certain or all foods. As already stated, animal food rather than vegetable, and meat rather than fish, and among meat that of the deer and elk, the largest of the game animals, were particularly subjected to restriction. In Northwestern California the idea was very deeply rooted that the deer when killed and eaten are not destroyed, but come to life again and report to their fellows their treatment in the hands of the hunter. Any violation of the numerous stringent observances regarding deer meat are therefore known to all the deer, who, as their capture is always a voluntary act on their part, are in position to utterly destroy his luck in the chase if not placated by certain spoken formulae. In Southern California young people, or in some cases the hunter himself, must not eat his game. Fasting is less frequently and less rigorously practiced by the California tribes than by those of most other parts of North America. This is in keeping with the generally lower pitch of intensity of their religious feeling. Many public ceremonies are not accompanied by any requirement of abstention from food. In the Northwestern region it is only the principal priest, in whom the most sacred part of the ceremony is vested, who fasts. On the other hand there is a general feeling in this region that not only acts of a religious nature but ordinary work cannot be well performed after eating. Among the men of Northwestern California breakfast was therefore habitually slight or entirely omitted. Perhaps the greatest development of the practice of fasting in North America occurs in connection with the acquisition of shamanistic power. Shamanism is fully as important among the California Indians as elsewhere, but differs in that it is more frequently regarded as an obsession, something that of its own accord comes upon a man rather than something that it is sought to acquire by actions. Much of the incentive for fasting among other Indians is therefore lacking, and when the practice is observed it is usually less rigorous. In Northwestern California, for instance, a person engaged in almost any supernatural or religious practice abstains from drinking water; but as to practical effect this provision is done away with through his being allowed to drink thin acorn soup at will.

In Northwestern California there is a special development of spoken formulae, whose content is little else than a myth and which constitute not only the basis and essential element of public ceremonies but are connected with almost all customary observances. To such an extent have these formulae, locally called "medicines," grown into the mind of these Indians as being what is most sacred and most efficacious in all aspects of religion, that they partly supplant shamanism, which is a less important feature of religious life here than elsewhere in the state, where the characteristic features of this peculiar ritual by formula are almost absent. Not only purification from death and other defilement, but luck in hunting and fishing, in gambling, escape from danger, success in felling trees and making baskets, in the acquisition of wealth, in short the proper achievement of every human wish, were thought to be accompanied by the proper knowledge and recitation of these traditional myth-formulae, usually accompanied by only the smallest amount of ritualistic action.

SHAMANISM.

Shamanism, the supposed individual control of the supernatural through a personally acquired power of communication with the spirit world, rests upon much the same basis in California as elsewhere in North America. In general among uncivilized tribes the simpler the stage of culture the more important the shaman. It is as if he constituted an element that remained nearly constant in quantity of effect, as it is fundamentally unvarying in form, through all successive periods of civilization to the highest; but that as increase in degree of civilization brought with it ever more and more new elements, religious and otherwise, and these unfolded in ever expanding complexity, he became, relatively to the total mass of thought and action of a people, less and less important. Certainly the difference is marked between the Eskimo, whose religion consists of little else than shamanism, and the much more highly organized Indians of the North Pacific Coast, where shamanism is but one of several and by no means the most important religious factor, even though it may be the most deep seated. The same contrast is found between the rude simple-minded Indians of California as compared with those of the Plains and of the Southwest, where the supremacy of the shaman is rather obscured by that of the priest conversant with a ceremony. Even within California the difference holds good. In the Northwest, where the native civilization reached on the whole its greatest complexity, the shaman is less prominent than anywhere else in the state. In the south, where the culture is also more developed than in the Central part of the state, the shaman is certainly as much dreaded as there; but that his province is more restricted is shown by the fact that in Southern California the shamans in their capacity as such do not seem to form associations, perform public ceremonies, or directly participate in the tribal dances.

The power of the shaman being directly dependent upon his personal acquisition of a connection with the supernatural world, an understanding of the method by which this acquisition takes place generally furnishes also a pretty accurate idea of the nature of his functions and influence. The most common way of acquiring shamanistic power in California, as in so many other parts of the world, is by dreaming. A spirit, be it that of an animal, a place, the sun or another natural object, a deceased relative, or an entirely unimbodied spirit, visits the future medicine-man in his dreams, and the connection thus established between them is the source and basis of the latter's power. This spirit becomes his guardian spirit or "personal." From it he receives the song or rite or knowledge of the charm and the understanding which enable him to cause or remove disease and to do and endure what other men cannot. In California, with a few special exceptions, the idea does not seem so prevalent as elsewhere that this guardian spirit is an animal. Occasionally it is the ghost of a person who has once lived, usually a relative. Perhaps most frequently it is merely a spirit as such, not connected with any tangible embodiment or form, either human, animate, or inanimate. The belief that the shaman acquires the spirits most frequently in dreaming is prevalent through the whole Sierra Nevada region and in many other parts of the state.

In certain regions another important method, that of the waking vision and trance, is recognized. The person is in a wild desolate place, perhaps hunting. Suddenly there is an appearance before him. He becomes unconscious and while in this state receives his supernatural power. On his return to his people he is for a time demented or physically affected. After he again becomes normal he has control of his supernatural influences. Such beliefs prevail in part among the Yuki and Athabascans of the Coast Range and the Maidu of the Sacramento valley, and no doubt occur more or less sporadically in other regions.

Finally, the shaman sometimes acquires his powers through seeking for them rather than by having them thrust upon him during a dream or vision. This of course is a common procedure in the Plains and in part on the North Pacific Coast. Among the Yurok of the lower Klamath, for instance, the person whom the spirits have visited in dreams, ascends high peaks where he spends one or more nights until he has acquired his powers. Among the Wiyot of Humboldt Bay there are similar beliefs. In the same Northwestern region a man who wishes to be fierce, strong, and invulnerable swims at night in lakes inhabited by monsters or thunders. From these, if his courage is sufficient to await and endure their presence, he receives the desired powers. This practice of bathing in lonely lakes closely recalls the custom prevalent along the Pacific slope for some distance northward, and within California it is probably not strictly confined to the Northwestern culture area. On the whole, however, this deliberate method of acquiring shamanistic power is not common, nor, as has already been stated, would it be in accord with the generally lower intensity of religious feeling among the California Indians as compared with those of most other parts of the continent.

The Northwestern area is not only exceptional in being the principal one within the state where this deliberate seeking of shamanistic power is prevalent. The conception of a guardian spirit is much less clearly defined among the Northwestern tribes, with whom the possession of "pains," the small material objects which cause disease, rather than of true spirits, seems to be what is generally associated with shamanistic power. As already stated, shamanism forms a much less important part of religion as a whole in the Northwestern area than elsewhere, and it is in accord with this fact that the majority of the shamans, and those supposed to be most powerful, are women.

In parts of Southern California also the idea of the guardian spirit does not seem to be well developed. Here the method of acquiring shamanistic power is almost exclusively by dreams; but among the Mohave and probably other Colorado river tribes, myths, and not a personal meeting or communion with an individual spirit, constitute the subject of the dreams. The Mohave shamans believe that they were present at the beginning of the world, before mankind had separated into tribes. They were with the great leader and almost creator, Mastamho. They saw him singing, blowing, and rubbing over the body of a sick man, if their own power be that of curing disease, and from Mastamho they thus learned the actions and speeches which constitute their power. Before him they showed what they had learned from him, and by him were designated those who had seen and learned most and those of less power. Each man saw only the shamanistic actions relating to his particular power, whether these had reference to the curing of disease, to love, to war, or to some other activity. The Mohave universally speak of having dreamed these scenes, just as each narrator affirms his knowledge of non-shamanistic myths and of ceremonies to have been individually derived from dreaming them. It is probable that to a certain extent this is true. That it is not entirely true becomes evident when the Mohave with equal unanimity state that these dreams were dreamed by them before birth. In other words, their statement that they have dreamed such experiences is to be interpreted mainly as a belief that they as individuals were present in spirit form at the beginning of the world, at the time when it took shape and everything was ordained, and when all power, shamanistic and otherwise, was established and allotted. It is obvious that with this conception as the basis of their whole religion, there is but little room for any beliefs as to guardian spirits of the usual form.

Of course there is nothing that limits the shaman to one spirit, and among many or most tribes, such as the Maidu, a powerful medicine-man may possess a great number.

Frequently in Central and Northwestern California there is some more or less public ceremony at which a new shaman is, so to speak, initiated before he practices his powers. The body of initiated shamans do not form a definite society or association. The ceremony is rather an occasion that marks the first public appearance of the novice, in which he receives for his own good, and presumably for that of the community also, the assistance of the more experienced persons of his profession. Commonly it is thought that the novice cannot receive and exercise the full use of his powers without this assistance. The ceremony is usually held in the ceremonial chamber and is accompanied by dancing. The efforts of the older shamans are directed toward giving the initiate a firm and permanent control of the spirits which have only half attached themselves to him and which are thought to be still more or less rebellious. Of course exhibitions of magic and of the physical effects of the presence of the spirits are a prominent feature of these ceremonies. This initiation of doctors is found among the Northwestern tribes and in the Central region among the Maidu and Wintun and probably other groups.

A special class of shamans found to a greater or less extent among probably all the Central tribes, though they are wanting both in the Northwest and the South, are the so-called bear doctors, shamans who have received power from grizzly bears, often by being taken into the abode of these animals—which appear there in human form,—and who after their return to mankind possess many of the qualities of the grizzly bear, especially his apparent invulnerability to fatal attack. The bear shamans can not only assume the form of bears, as they do in order to inflict vengeance on their enemies, but it is believed that they can be killed an indefinite number of times when in this form and each time return to life. In some regions, as among the Pomo and Yuki, the bear shaman was not thought as elsewhere to actually become a bear, but to remain a man who clothed himself in the skin of a bear to his complete disguisement, and by his malevolence, rapidity, fierceness, and resistance to wounds to be capable of inflicting greater injury than a true bear. Whether any bear shamans actually attempted to disguise themselves in this way to accomplish their ends is doubtful. It is certain that all the members of some tribes believed it to be in their power.

The rattlesnake doctor, who cured or prevented the bite of the rattlesnake, was usually distinct from other medicine-men. Among the Yuki his power, as that of the rattlesnake, was associated with the sun; among the Maidu with the thunder. Among the Yokuts the rattlesnake shamans annually held a public ceremony designed to prevent rattlesnake bites among the tribe. On this occasion they displayed their power over the snakes by handling them in a manner analogous to that of the Hopi, and by even allowing themselves to be bitten.

As everywhere else, the practice of shamanism in California centers about disease and death. It is probably more narrowly limited to this phase than in most other portions of North America. Being an essentially unwarlike even though a revengeful people, it is natural that the supernatural power personally acquired by the California Indian should not often be directed toward success in battle. Success in love is also less often the result of such personal power than for instance on the Plains, perhaps because in the latter region the custom which made virtually every young man seek shamanistic power, resulted in a condition where those whose proclivities were not toward medicine or war, desired and received their powers in this direction. Influence over game and over nature's yield of vegetable products was sometimes attributed to shamans in California, but on the whole their powers in this respect were not very much insisted upon except in Southern California, favorable or adverse conditions of this kind being attributed rather to the tribal ceremonies, and in the Northwest connected with the all-important formulae. The causing and prevention of disease and death were therefore even more largely the predominant functions of the person who had acquired personal supernatural power in California than elsewhere in America.

That the medicine-men who could cure diseases were also the ones who must cause it, unless it were the direct consequence of an infraction of some religious observance or prohibition, was the almost universal belief, which was probably adhered to with greater definiteness than in most portions of North America. The killing of medicine-men was therefore of frequent occurrence. Among some tribes, as the Yokuts, the medicine-man who had lost several patients was held responsible for their death by their relatives. Among the Mohave also murder seems to have been the normal end of the medicine-man. In the Northwestern region the shaman who failed to cure was forced to return the fee received in advance. If he refused to attend a patient when summoned, he was compelled to pay, in the event of the latter's death, an amount of property equal that proffered him for his services. So completely was the shaman regarded as the cause of disease and death, as well as of their prevention, that one hears very little among the California Indians of witchcraft, that is to say, of malevolent practices performed by persons, often very old or very young people, who are not believed to be endowed with the shaman's power of curing.

Disease, as among most primitive peoples the world over, was usually held to be caused by small material objects which had in a supernatural way been caused to enter the body. The determination and extraction of these was the principal office of the medicine-man and, also as elsewhere, was most frequently accomplished by sucking. In certain regions, especially the South, the tubular pipe was brought into requisition for this purpose, the disease-object being supposed to be sucked into the doctor's mouth through it. Among such tribes the pipe was also smoked by the medicine-man as part of his ritual. In other cases the sucking was performed directly with the mouth, but, just as the disease-causing object had by supernatural means entered the body without causing or leaving an opening, so it was extracted by the medicine-man without an incision or a trace of its passage. This object might be a bit of hair, a stick, an insect or small reptile, a piece of bone, deer sinew, or almost any other material. In the greater part of northern California, including the Northwestern region, it was not an ordinary physical object working mischief by its mere presence in the body or by the supernatural properties with which the shaman or his spirits had endowed it, but an object itself supernatural and called a "pain." These pains are variously described, frequently as being sharp at both ends and clear as ice. They possessed the power of moving even after extracted, and were able to fly through the air to the intended victim at the command of the person who had sent them. The medicine-man after extracting the disease-object or pain almost always exhibited it. It was then either destroyed by him or kept by him for his own use. In Northwestern California he sometimes swallowed it, the degree of his power being thought to be dependent upon the number of pains he kept in his body, both those which he received upon his becoming a shaman, when they were "cooked" before a great fire in the doctor-initiation dance, and those which he subsequently secured in doctoring his patients. The rattlesnake's bite was regarded as being dangerous on account of its injection into the victim's body of a material animate object, which the rattlesnake shaman must extract if death was not to ensue. Among the Yuki this object was a small snake; among the Yokuts a rodent's tooth or other object supposed to have formed part of the animals upon which the snake subsisted. In some cases two classes of medicine-men were distinguished, one diagnosing, the other treating the patient. Among the Wiyot or Wishosk the former by dancing before the patient saw in a vision the nature and location of the disease-object and determined what had caused it to enter the body. Somewhat similar though varying distinctions between shamans whose power consists of knowledge, and those who have practical capacity as well, occurred among other tribes. Sucking is not always resorted to. The Mohave principally blow or spit over their patients and stroke or rub or knead their bodies, which actions are supposed by them to drive out the disease. Medicines and drugs are but little used, or if so, in a manner that gives no opportunity for their physiological efficacy. Four or five drops —the number varying according to the ceremonial number of the tribe—of a weak decoction may be given to the patient or even only applied to him externally. It is natural that where the magic effect of the drug as used in a certain ritual is believed in, the quantity so used is not an essential consideration. It is the supernatural qualities connected with the plant that bring about the desired result, and these are as inherent in a drop placed upon the forehead as in a basketful taken internally. Perhaps the most-used medicinal plant throughout the state is the angelica root, probably principally on account of its fragrance. Tobacco is considerably employed by shamans, but is of equal importance in other aspects of religion.

PUBLIC CEREMONIES.

After the exclusion of such public observances as the shaman initiation, menstrual dance, and victory celebration, which, while generally participated in, are performed primarily for the benefit of individuals, the ceremonies of the California Indians which are of a really public or communal purpose and character fall into three classes: (1) mourning ceremonies; (2) initiation ceremonies connected with a secret society; and (3) a more varied group of dances and other observances which all, however, have in common the benefit either of the community or of the world at large, in that they cause a good crop of acorns and natural products, make the avoidance of rattlesnake bites possible, or prevent the occurrence of disease, earthquake, flood, and other calamities.

Of these three classes of ceremonies the mourning ceremonies are at least as important as the others and by far the most distinctive of the state as an ethnographic province, although neither they nor the secret society are found in the specialized Northwestern area. The mourning ceremonies further do not occur among the Athabascan, Yuki, and Pomo tribes to the south of the Northwestern tribes as far as the bay of San Francisco; but outside of this strip in the northern coast region they are universal in the state. Among the Maidu they are usually known as "burning," among the Miwok as "cry." Among the Yokuts they have been called "dance of the dead," and among the Mohave and Yuma "annual." These ceremonies are usually participated in by a number of visiting communities or villages. They last for one or more nights, during which crying and wailing, sometimes accompanied by singing and exhortation, are indulged in, and find their climax in a great destruction of property. While those who have recently lost relatives naturally take a prominent part, the ceremony as a whole is not a personal but a tribal one. Among the Yokuts and probably other groups it is immediately followed by a dance of a festive nature, and usually there is a definitely expressed idea that this general ceremony puts an end to all individual mourning among the participants. A typical form of the mourning ceremony is found among the Maidu, who call it östu. Each village or political unit possesses its burning ground. Participation in the ceremony is effected by receipt of a membership-string or necklace, both the receipt and return of which are marked by payments or presents. The ceremony is held in autumn in a circular brush enclosure. Property to be destroyed is tied to poles which are erected on the ground. After an opening exhortation by the chief or shaman in charge of the ceremony, the wailing begins, to continue throughout the night, many exclamations to the dead being uttered. Toward morning the numerous articles displayed on the poles are taken down and burned. When everything has been destroyed the assembly breaks up for gambling and feasting. The purpose of the ceremony is to supply the ghosts of the dead with clothing, property, and food. Although its general tenor is communal, each family offers only to its own relatives. In some cases elaborate images of stuffed skins ornamented with dancing apparel are made to represent important people who have died. These are burned with the property offered to the dead.

Initiation ceremonies which result in something analogous to a secret society are found in the whole state except in the Northwestern region and among the agricultural tribes at the extreme southeast in the Colorado valley. They are apparently as well developed among the Yuki and Pomo, who do not practice tribal mourning ceremonies, as among their neighbors who do. In a strict sense there is no secret society, even though the precepts taught boys at initiation are not made public. There are usually no paraphernalia or insignia of a society, no degrees or ranks, no membership or other organization, nor is there a definite purpose for the society. The great majority of the males of the tribes are made to undergo the initiation, and in many cases there is a distinct desire to force it upon every man, whether he be willing or unwilling. In so far as a society may therefore be said to exist at all, its principal purpose and public function are the initiation of new members. There is however often a special name for those who have been initiated, such as yeponi among the Maidu and pumal among the Luiseño, and to a certain extent the initiates are regarded as a class or council having a more or less indefinite decision over religious matters affecting the community. The precepts imparted to the initiates, other than the ritualistic knowledge relating to the initiation ceremony itself, seems to be of the most general kind and pertains principally to daily life and the most obvious maxims of native morality. In some ways this initiation is a puberty ceremony for boys corresponding to the first-menstruation-ceremony of girls. The initiates are however not limited as to age, men being sometimes included. Among at least the Yokuts in Central California and the Mission Indians of Southern California the initiation was accompanied by the drinking of toloache or jimson-weed, datura meteloides, the stupor and visions produced by which were regarded as supernatural. In Southern California the idea of an ordeal and instruction was specially developed. Boys were made to undergo severe tests of pain and endurance and were given numerous injunctions regarding their adult life. Among the Maidu of the Sacramento valley instruction both in the myths of the tribe and in the more important ceremonies was imparted. Among certain of the Maidu the secret society, in so far as it comprises the more adult men, is difficult to distinguish from an association of shamans.

The public ceremonies other than mourning and initiation observances, in other words the tribal dances of California, differ thoroughly in the three culture regions, which must therefore be considered separately.

In Central California these dances, like the initiation ceremonies, have disappeared to a much greater extent than the mourning ceremonies, and where they survive have often been more or less influenced by modern ideas. As a rule they were held in the large assembly or ceremonial chamber, more often at night than during the day, and either lasted for a number of nights or consisted of a series of successive dances extending over a considerable period. Some of the dances, though a minority, were named after animals, and in such there was usually some imitation of the actions of animals. Sometimes rude paraphernalia were used to represent the animal itself, but this was not very common and masks were never employed. At least in the Sacramento valley and northern Coast Range region there was some impersonation of mythical characters, as of Taikomol, creator among the Yuki, and of the mythical being Kuksu among the Pomo and Maidu. Such impersonators usually wore either the "big head," an enormous head-dress of feathers attached to radiating sticks, or a large cape of feathers fastened to a network, which concealed both body and face, or both pieces of apparel. There seems to have been nothing corresponding to an altar. The dancers were painted but crudely, and such symbolism as was denoted by the painting was of the simplest. One or more of the posts that supported the roof of the assembly chamber were usually of ceremonial importance. The dancers frequently entered and left the house by a hole above instead of the door at the ground. A rude drum consisting of a hollow slab placed on the ground and stamped with the feet was often used. An important character in most ceremonies was the clown or buffoon, part of whose duties was to caricature the more serious performance. In some cases shamanistic exhibitions of magic were included in the ceremony. At times an exchange or compulsory giving of property formed part of the ceremony. The participants were rarely if ever called upon to undergo severe trials of endurance, pain, or courage, as among so many other Indians. The whole ritual was comparatively simple.

The exact nature and relation of the various dances are very little known among most of the tribes of the Central region. Probably a typical example of these dances is furnished by the Maidu of the Sacramento valley, who declare that their ceremonies were obtained from their neighbors, the Wintun. This statement is borne out by indirect evidence. Among the Maidu the ceremonies were performed in winter and constituted a series of fifteen or more distinct dances, coming for the most part in a definite order. So far as known they were the following: Hesi, Luyi, Loli, Salalu-ngkasi, Duck, Bear, Coyote, Creeper, Turtle, Aloli-ngkasi, Yokola-ngkasi, Moloko-ngkasi, Deer, Aki, Hesi. The majority of these dances were performed by men, but some by women only. There is no evidence that participation in these dances was dependent upon anything like membership in an association. Each had its characteristic paraphernalia or combinations of paraphernalia. In several there are participants with special apparel and with a distinctive name. At least some of these seem to represent mythical characters. In several instances these performers enact ceremonial operations, largely in the nature of complex approaches and departures which take place outside the assembly chamber. The names of several of these ceremonies occur also among neighboring Indians speaking entirely different languages, and thus give proof of the transmission of the ceremonies from one locality to another. The Hesi, the most important of the Maidu series, is danced also by the Wintun. The Loli is an important ceremony among the Maidu, Miwok, and Pomo. The performer called Kuksu, who refers to important myths, is found among the Maidu, Wintun, Pomo, and either the Miwok or Costanoan Indians formerly at Mission San José. There is every reason to believe that a fuller acquaintance with the tribes whose ceremonies are as yet least known will reveal other instances of ceremonies held in common and known under the same name. Farther to the south, among the Yokuts of the

Tulare basin, these ceremonies do not seem to have penetrated. Here the majority of the public ceremonies, like the rattlesnake ceremony that has been mentioned, were of the nature of shamanistic performances. Throughout the Central region the dances, while they might be held only in structures of certain kinds, were never rigorously attached to a specific locality.

In Northwestern California the more important ceremonies can always be held only at certain spots, and the performance of ceremonies of the same name always varies somewhat at different places. The performers do not represent mythological or other characters and do not imitate animals. The more important dances last at least a number of days, not infrequently as many as ten. The dances are held either out-doors or in certain sacred houses, which are however not different from the ordinary living-house of the region except through their traditionary and ceremonial associations. The essential religious portion of the ceremony consists of the actions gone through by a priest, with sometimes one or two assistants. The more important part of his procedure is the recital of one of the sacred formulae so characteristic of the region. This formula relates specifically to the exact locality at which the dance is held, and therefore often varies considerably from spot to spot. The formula is regarded as it were as private property, and its knowledge is sufficient to institute the priest in his capacity. The public portions of the ceremony, such as the dancing, are practically dissociated from this purely religious element. The dancers are mostly young men without any knowledge of the ceremony other than of the simple dance-step and songs. The paraphernalia which they wear belong neither to them nor to the priests, but to wealthy men of the tribe, for whom the occasion is an all-important opportunity for the display of their wealth, which consists in large part of the dancing regalia, and the possession of which is the chief factor toward their social prominence. The dancers appear in from two to five parties, representing neighboring villages, each of which is aided by the wealthy men of other villages; and these parties vie with each other primarily in the display of their regalia. The most important ceremonies are the Deerskin dance and the Jumping dance, which are held either annually or biennially, the former always out-doors, the latter at some places out-doors, sometimes in boats, at others in-doors. The purpose of both dances, which where both are practiced are usually given in close succession, is the good of the world. Earthquake and disease are prevented and a food supply insured. Very little of the sacred formulae and accompanying ritual, and nothing in the remainder of the dance, has however any specific reference to this purpose. A third, minor ceremony, the Brush dance, completes the series of public ceremonies in this region, the remaining dances being held only on occasion of war, a girl's puberty, or the initiation of a shaman. Even the Brush dance is not fully of a tribal character, inasmuch as it is performed for the benefit of a single individual, a sick child, although it is participated in by an entire village with the assistance of visitors from others, and though there seems to be a desire to perform the ceremony at least once a year in each of the larger villages.

In Southern California mourning ceremonies are everywhere the most prominent. In the coast region, among the various groups of Mission Indians, initiation ceremonies make up most of the public rituals that are not connected with mourning. In the interior the Mohave possess no initiation ceremonies. In both regions such ceremonies as partake neither of the nature of mourning nor initiation are conspicuous by the prominence of the myth element. They consist essentially of long series of songs, occupying one or more nights in the recital, which recount, in part directly but more often by allusion, an important myth. At times the myth is actually related in the intervals between the songs. In some cases dancing by men or women accompanies the singing, but this is never spectacular and in many cases is entirely lacking. Being only ceremonial recitations of myths, these ceremonies are not attached in their performance to specific localities, and when dancing regalia are used they are of the simplest character; nor is there opportunity for either altar or ritual. The predominance of the mourning element in the ceremonies of this region is further shown by the fact that among some tribes, as the Mohave, these same singing ceremonies, besides being performed independently, are also sung for many hours at every death. The series of songs selected for each individual on this occasion is that with which he is acquainted. In accord with what has been said of the dream as the basis of Mohave religious life, these singing ceremonies are almost always believed by each person to have been dreamed by himself.

CEREMONIAL STRUCTURES AND PARAPHERNALIA.

The ceremonial chamber is also of distinctive character in the three culture areas. In the Central region it is a large, circular, dome-shaped structure, partly underground and with a covering of earth. It serves also as place of assembly and at least at times as sudatory, whence its popular name of sweat-house. In the Northwest the sweat-house is quite small, almost entirely underground, and its roof consists of boards without a covering of earth. It is constantly used for sweating and is the regular sleeping place of all adult males. It is not used for public ceremonies except in the case of the dance initiating shamans. In the South the ceremonial structure is not a house, but either a mere enclosure of brush, as among the Mission tribes, or a simple shade of brush on upright posts, as among the Mohave. This type of ceremonial structure is also found in the southern part of the Central region among the Yokuts.

In the matter of dancing apparel the Northwest differs fundamentally from all the remainder of the state. Some of the most important of the regalia, such as long obsidian knives and albino deerskins, are not worn on the body or used ritually but merely carried for display, being primarily objects of great value. Large forehead-bands entirely covered with brilliant red woodpecker feathers more nearly resemble ordinary dancing apparel, but are also articles of value, the unmounted woodpecker feathers virtually constituting one form of currency. Other objects used in dancing are dresses, cloaks, and head-bands of skin and fur, head-dresses of network, and carefully ornamented plumes and head feathers. All these, while worn on the body, and decorative, also possess considerable commercial value. The drum is not used, the whistle employed at times, and the rattle, which consists of deer hoofs, but sparingly.

In the Central region objects made of feathers greatly predominate over all others, and are mostly made to be worn actually on the body. Head-dresses are particularly conspicuous and of many forms. In the Sacramento and San Joaquin valleys and the adjacent region cloaks of large feathers attached to a network are worn. In the Tulare basin these are replaced by skirts consisting of strings of eagle-down. With these down-skirts are worn large upright head-dresses of crow and magpie feathers. This combination of costume was used also by the Mission Indians in Southern California and by the Washo of Nevada, and at least the head-dress is found as far north as the Sacramento valley. Network caps filled with down, and forehead bands of down, are frequent in various parts. Perhaps the most typical single object of ceremonial apparel is a flat band, usually worn on the forehead, and consisting of the trimmed red quills of the yellow-hammer sewed side by side. This head-band occurs through the whole of Central California and is used also by the tribes east of the Sierra Nevada, in the state of Nevada, and south of Tehachapi pass in Southern California. The large foot drum of the Central region has already been mentioned. Whistles are also used and there are two forms of rattle, one consisting of silk cocoons containing gravel, the other of a split stick. The cocoon rattle is usually associated with the shaman, the clap-stick with dancing.

In the South, especially among the Mission Indians, the dancing apparel, as is evident from the instances already mentioned, is of much the same type as in the Central area. On the Colorado river feather ornaments of the same general character are used, though they are of a simpler type and head-dresses predominate. The whistle is but little used in the South, the drum occasionally, baskets and other objects being chiefly employed for this purpose. The rattle is the all-important musical instrument in this region. It is made most frequently from a gourd or a turtle-shell.

MYTHOLOGY AND BELIEFS.

In mythology a deep-going difference between the three culture areas again appears. The Northwestern mythologies are characterized primarily by a very deeply impressed conception of a previous, now vanished, race, who by first living the life and performing the actions of mankind were the producers of all human institutions and arts as well as of some of the phenomena of nature. Second in importance in the Northwest are myths dealing with culture-heroes more or less of the trickster type familiar from so many other parts of North America.

In Central California there is always a true creation of the world, of mankind, and of its institutions. The conception of the creator is often quite lofty, and tricky exploits or defeats are usually not connected with him. Often there is an antithesis between this beneficent and truly divine creator and a second character, usually the Coyote, who in part coöperates with the creator but in part thwarts him, being responsible for the death of mankind and other imperfections in the world-scheme. In the northern half of the Central region the creator is generally anthropomorphic; if not, he is merged into one personage with the more or less tricky Coyote. In the southern half of the region the creators seem always to be animals with the dignified and wise eagle as the chief. The myths of the Central region not directly concerned with creation are mostly stories of adventure, of much the same type as European folk and fairy tales. They do not explain the origin of phenomena except in a casual, isolated way, and but rarely are of ceremonial import.

In Southern California there is no creation. The various animate and inanimate existences in the world are born from heaven and earth as the first parents. Sometimes heaven and earth are regarded as the first concrete existences, who were, however, preceded by a series of psychic beings grouped in pairs. The bulk of the Southern origin myth consists of a history of mankind, at first as a single tribe and later centered in the tribe which tells the story. In the successive experiences of this body of people, which are accompanied by more or less journeying, the world is gradually brought to its present stage, and all the institutions of mankind, particularly of the narrating tribe but also of others, are developed. The people are under the leadership of one or two great leaders, at least one of whom always dies or departs after his beneficent directions. The thoroughly Southwestern and Pueblo character of this long origin myth is obvious. It is usually followed to a greater or less extent by migration legends recounting the wandering and conflicts of different tribes or clans. The remaining myths are in plot essentially not very different from the adventure stories of the Central region, but both much longer and more elaborate, and at the same time distinctively ritualistic in that they form the basis or framework of the singing ceremonies that have been described. As these ceremonies themselves are nothing but myths, there is neither need nor room for traditionary accounts explaining the origin of the ceremonies.

An identification of myth and ceremony that is in many ways similar to that prevalent in Southern California is characteristic also of the Northwestern region, where the formulae which constitute the essential religious elements, as well as being the direct means, of most supernatural accomplishment, are nothing but myths. The Northwestern formula is a myth, rarely a direct prayer, and practically every more serious myth is either in whole or in part also a formula. In purpose, however, as well as in rendering, the spoken myth-formulae of the Northwest and the sung myth-ceremonies of the South are different, the former having always a definite practical result in view, whereas the latter have no aim other than their own recital.

Thus the mythology of Southern California resembles that of the Southwest rather than that of the remainder of the state. That of the Northwestern region shows affinities to the North Pacific Coast in its prevalence of the culture-hero and trickster over the creator. The most marked special characteristic of the Northwestern mythology, other than its practical use of myths for religious purposes in the shape of formulas, is its strong and definite, though inconsistently carried out, idea of the previous race which is parallel to but distinct from mankind, and which is the originator, not by any act of creation but by merely living its life, of everything human except mankind itself, the origin of which is never accounted for. This idea of a previous supernatural race analogous to mankind crops out to some extent in almost all North American mythologies, and particularly in other parts of California; but it seems nowhere to be so deep-seated and so freely expressed as in this region. The members of this vanished race are almost always strictly human, in Northwestern

California, and not animals or personifications. They are nothing but men, living the life of the Indians, transposed into a mythic supernatural age, and by the fact of their mere existence regarded as the originators of the present condition of the world. They therefore leave no room for a creator, and but little for the culture hero, whose exploits, when not of purely personal significance, consequently consist mainly of the destruction of evil beings.

If the mythology of Northwestern California in spite of its partial northern affinities accordingly has a dominant character all its own, the same is also true of the larger, more representative Central region. A true creator, and a full and consistent attempt at an account of the creation, are found nowhere else in North America, or at least only sporadically and carried out with an apparently much less degree of thoroughness. The remainder of the Central Californian mythology however scarcely presents any unique qualities, even some of the specific myth-episodes, such as the favorite one of the bear and deer children, being found over considerable territories outside of California. Even the important characteristic of the presence of creation-myths is in a measure a negative one, for from a world view some approach to such a myth may be expected among most peoples, whether primitive or civilized, and it is primarily only in America that special bents of mind and of religious thought have supplanted the idea of creation by the culture hero, the tribal history, and other conceptions. We are therefore not far from right if we regard the unique development of creation myths over the greater part of California as merely a part of a general tendency of the California Indians towards simplicity and lack of strongly marked peculiar and American qualities in any one direction, a tendency which has already been emphasized in other aspects of their religion, and which must be said to characterize their whole life and culture.

Ideas as to the world and the existence of the dead vary from tribe to tribe but present nothing specially distinctive. The world is usually regarded as surrounded by water, sometimes as floating upon it. It is often secured by four or five pillars, ropes, or other supports. Beyond where earth and sky meet there is often another land. The dead sometimes go below, sometimes above, sometimes across the ocean to the west, and sometimes to more or less distant parts of this earth. The entrance to the world of the dead is pointed out by some tribes. People who have temporarily died have been there and returned to describe it. Dances constitute the principal occupation of the dead. No ideas of future rewards and punishments based on conduct in this life have yet been found. If such ideas exist they must be very scantily developed. As in other parts of the world, there are occasional ideas of transmigration of souls into animals, but these conceptions are nowhere systematically worked out or of any religious importance.

SPECIAL CHARACTERISTICS OF DIFFERENT TRIBES.

Such are the principal characteristics of the religion of the Indians of California as a whole, and of the larger ethnographical areas of the state. It is obvious that with so great a linguistic and political diversification as existed among these Indians, there must have been many local modifications of the scheme which has been outlined. The most conspicuous or best known of these special modifications it is the purpose of the remainder of this paper to consider. In this review the groups to be taken up will, for the sake of greatest convenience of classification, be the linguistic families. These numerous families are territorially so restricted, and usually so small in numbers, that they almost form the equivalent of the tribe in other regions of North America, that is to say, of a subdivision of the family. Strictly there are no tribes in the greater part of California. The families or stocks are the largest linguistic units, usually subdivided into several dialectic areas, each of which contains a number of small village communities that are the only units of political or social organization.

In the Northwestern region, in spite of the excessive limitation of this territory, a distinction must be made between three tribes which occupy the heart of the region and show the culture in its most extreme form, and a fringe of surrounding tribes where the Northwestern culture is either less developed or subject to greater extraneous influences. The three more characteristic groups are the Yurok and Karok, small independent linguistic families, and the Hupa division of the Athabascan family. These alone practice the Deerskin dance and the "New Year's" or world-making ceremonies. With them also the peculiar mythological and shamanistic conceptions typical of the region are found in the purest form. The surrounding tribes are the Wishosk or Wiyot, perhaps the Chimariko and some of the Shasta, the Athabascan Tolowa, and the Athabascans southwest of the Hupa.

The Yurok held the Deerskin and Jumping dances at three places along the Klamath river, and the Jumping dance alone at three points on the coast to the south. At the mouth of the river an annual spring ceremony to cause or regulate the ascent of the salmon was made. Until this ceremony had been made salmon were not eaten. The shamans of the Yurok were almost all women. Alone of all the tribes in the Northwestern region the Yurok held no dance or public ceremony on the occasion of a girl's puberty. Their traditions seem to have the peculiar Northwestern qualities perhaps more deeply impressed upon them than even those of their neighbors, the Karok and Hupa, especially in regard to the underlying conception of a previous race and its function. In accord with the development of this conception, the mythical heroes of the Yurok show less approximation to being creators than those of the other tribes, and animals are mentioned in the mythology surprisingly little.

The Karok, who live immediately upstream from the Yurok on the Klamath, held the Deerskin and Jumping dances at three places. At each of these the dances were conducted in connection with a sacred ceremony called "New Year's" by the whites and "making the world" by the Indians. This ceremony was performed early in autumn, practically by one man, the priest who knew the formula and ritual. A similar ceremony was held at a fourth locality in spring, in connection with the coming of the salmon. The Karok regard the Deerskin and Jumping dances of the Yurok and Hupa as the equivalents of these ceremonies of their own, reckoning altogether ten places in the world at which they are performed. Karok mythology is of the Northwestern type, but shows more animal characters than that of the Yurok.

The territory held by the Hupa was much less extended than that of their neighbors, and this was no doubt the occasion of their making only one Deerskin and Jumping dance in their valley. They held a New Year's ceremony in autumn which had distinct reference to the acorn crop. Ceremonials and restrictions connected with menstruation were considerably developed, much more than among the neighboring Yurok. It was thought dangerous to speak to a dog, as he might be provoked to answer, which would be a fatal portent.

The religion of the other Athabascans in this part of the state is very little known, but it is certain that before the southern end of Humboldt county is reached, in other words, in the Eel river drainage, a totally distinct set of conceptions and practices is encountered, which are allied to those of the Central region.

The Wiyot or Wishosk, who adjoin the Yurok on the south, did not practice the Jumping dance, other ceremonies, which are very little known, taking its place among them. One dance was performed by women standing up to the hips in water. Shamanism is of more prominence among them than with their neighbors the Yurok, and men as well as women are affected with supernatural powers. The sex of the guardian spirit is usually the opposite of that of the shaman. It is possible that on account of the almost complete disappearance of their tribal life and communal religious practices, shamanism, which has been retained with greater vigor among the Wiyot, now appears relatively more important, as the only remnant of the religious side of their culture. An elaborate hanging feather head-dress, a belt, a pipe for smoking, and another for sucking, are the constant paraphernalia of the medicine-man. Two shamans often support each other in curing disease, one diagnosing, the other removing the pain. The mythology of the Wiyot resembles that of the Yurok chiefly through possessing certain specific narrative episodes in common with it. But the idea of a previous parallel race is very little developed, and there is a true creator, Above-Old-Man. Most of the other mythical characters are animals. The whole mythology therefore is of the Central rather than of the Northwestern type.

With the Yuki of Mendocino county a pure form of the

Central culture obtains. The creator is Taikomol, "he who goes alone." His companion, who supplements his work, especially as regards the culture of man, is Coyote. There is a Taikomol ceremony in which this character is impersonated, and which is shamanistic at least to the degree of being performed to cure an individual of sickness. There is no trace of the sacred formulae of the Northwest. The shaman, who is usually a man, receives his power either by dreaming or in a vision in a desolate place. His power is not sought by him and he possesses definite guardian spirits. Bear shamans are much feared. All the Yuki possess a sacred society initiation ceremony, in which performances of magic are prominent. Among the northern Yuki and neighboring Wailaki this is called Flint ceremony, and the initiates display magic powers in handling and swallowing flint points. Among the southern Yuki, as among the neighboring Pomo and Athabascan Kato, the ceremony relates to ghosts and is popularly known as Devil dance. The members possess power of causing sickness and contend against each other much like the shamans of the Maidu and Yokuts.

One of the most conspicuous features of the religion of the Pomo, who are south of the Yuki, is their shamanistic fetishes. The medicine-man possesses a number of objects, stones, parts of animals, and other articles, which he treasures and with which his power is largely bound up. Pomo mythology is characterized by the importance of Coyote, who comes nearer than any other personage to playing the part of creator. In certain ceremonies there are exhibitions of fire-eating and the clown occurs.

The Wintun occupy a territory which is of much greater extent from north to south than from east to west. The northern and southernmost members of the family therefore differ considerably. In the north there is a well defined conception of a creator who dwells above, and to whom Coyote forms an antithesis. In the south, where everything shows the Wintun and Pomo to have influenced each other considerably, he is replaced by Coyote. In both regions a world-fire is prominent in the mythology. In the north the shaman is inaugurated in his career in a ceremony in which he is assisted by his older colleagues. The southern Wintun may prove to have been the people who largely developed the dances and ceremonies characteristic of a large part of the Sacramento valley. They show much in common with their western neighbors the Pomo, and with the Maidu who adjoin them on the east and who themselves declare that they have derived the Hesi and other dances from them.

None of the groups so far discussed, with the possible exception of part of the Wintun, practiced any distinct mourning ceremony. On the other hand, all that follow, with the possible doubtful exception of one or two tribes on the outskirts of the state, held mourning ceremonies as among the most important of all their religious practices.

The Maidu everywhere possessed a secret society. Their system of dances becomes less and less developed as one proceeds farther from Wintun influence. Among the mountain tribes almost all ceremonies were much less developed than in the Sacramento valley. Shamanistic beliefs and practices also varied, although there was everywhere a clear idea of spirits personally acquired and controlled by the medicine-man. Among the northeastern Maidu every shaman's son invariably became a shaman, although only through his own acquisition of spirits, which might be those of his father. In the Sacramento valley spirits were acquired by involuntary dreaming without much regard to heredity. Puberty ceremonies for girls were performed both among the northwestern and northeastern Maidu, perhaps among those of the south also. The mythology of the several Maidu divisions is much more uniform than their religious practices. The creator is always opposed and his beneficent work rendered incomplete by Coyote. It is clear that the mythology of the Maidu is distinctive and much less under Wintun influence than their ceremonies.

Among the Miwok the Coyote largely takes the place of the creator. As among their northern neighbors the Maidu, the mourning ceremony was important, and the two stocks held at least certain dances in common. The individual mourning practices and restrictions of the widow were elaborate and severe. Nothing is as yet known of a secret society, but as both the southern and northern neighbors of the Miwok performed initiation ceremonies, it is likely that they also possessed them.

Among the Yokuts, who occupied the head of the San Joaquin-Tulare valley south of the Miwok, there are no traces of the ceremonial system of the Sacramento valley, which is replaced by public shamanistic ceremonies, in which contests and exhibitions of magic were conspicuous. The annual rattlesnake ceremony which has been described is of this type, as is the Ohowish, a ceremony in which medicine-men from different villages or districts directed their powers against each other. There seem to have been also certain animal dances among the Yokuts. Medicine-men usually acquired their power by dreaming, sometimes by visions while alone. Bear shamans were known, but were not so much dreaded as farther north. Rain doctors, who could control the weather, were important. Their power was bound up with certain stone amulets evidencing a fetishistic development. Formulae, some with ritualistic accompaniment, were spoken, but differed from those of the Northwest in being short direct prayers or supplications instead of mythical narratives. The creators in Yurok mythology are several animals, the chief of whom is the eagle and among whom Coyote always finds a place. A favorite mythological personage is the prairie-falcon, and a myth which has found a particular development relates the visit of a husband to the world of the dead in pursuit of his wife.

Very little is known of the ethnology of the coast tribes west of the Miwok and Yokuts. Among the Southern Costanoan peoples creation myths resembling those of the Yokuts are found. Coyote is at once a trickster and a giver of civilization and arts to man. Similar ideas probably prevailed among the Salinan tribes. As regards the Esselen and Chumash nothing is known.

Tribes belonging to the great Shoshonean family held almost all the eastern border of the state as well as a large part of the southern desert and coast region. The former inhabited the Great Basin, and are culturally entirely distinct from those of Southern California, of whom alone is there any considerable knowledge extant as regards religion. Certain of the northern groups, such as the Mono, lived on the western or California slope of the Sierra Nevada, in contact with the Yokuts and Miwok, and partook more largely of the culture and presumably religion of these people than of the tribes of the Basin.

Among the Shoshoneans of Southern California, such as the Gabrielino and Luiseño, the so-called Mission Indians, mourning ceremonies were more important than any others, and were held both on the death of a person, sometime afterwards, and again in a still more public manner at large gatherings. At some of these ceremonies images representing the dead, and recalling those of the Maidu far to the north, were burned. One form of mourning ceremony was the Eagle dance, performed with an eagle that was slowly killed as the ceremony went on through the night. Many of the songs of the mourning ceremonies are of mythological content, referring to the great leader or culture-hero Wiyot. The puberty ceremonial for girls was elaborate and contained symbolic actions. The initiation of males was intended for boys, and therefore also took on largely the character of a puberty ceremony. This character was heightened by the presence of numerous ordeals. Part of the initiation of boys consisted of the drinking of jimson-weed. Sand paintings of a very simple type, evidently influenced by basket patterns, but thoroughly symbolic in meaning and therefore essentially of the same nature as those of the Pueblos and Navaho, were made in connection with this initiation. On the whole religious symbolism was more developed than in Central California or even among the Yuman tribes to the east, who are geographically so much nearer the Indians of the Southwest. The shaman acquired his power by dreaming, and the pipe with which he sucked as well as smoked was of the utmost importance to him. Paraphernalia were much used by the shamans, especially boards or wooden swords, which were swallowed and worn as head-dresses. These, however, were not purely fetishistic objects, but of potency rather through symbolism and association. The mythology of the Shoshonean Mission Indians was not essentially different from that of the other Indians of Southern California.

The Yuman family, which is so much represented in Arizona and Lower California, occupied the southernmost portion of Southern California. The Diegueño in the coast mountains and on the coast were culturally similar to the Shoshonean Luiseño, with whom they are generally included as the present Mission Indians. Along the Colorado river the physical and ethnic environment was quite different, but as has already been said, there was much closer resemblance to the Mission Indians in matters of religion than in almost any other phase of culture. The principal Yuman tribes in this Colorado region are the Mohave and the Yuma. The religion of only the former is known, but the two give every evidence of having been very similar. The religion of the Shoshonean Paiute or Chemehuevi in the desert adjoining the Mohave has been largely colored by the influence of the latter. The most distinctive feature of Mohave religion is the insistence upon dreaming as the source of everything religious, although this dreaming must be interpreted rather as a belief in the presence of the individual in spirit form at the great events of mythic times. All myths that are at all of sacred character are believed not to be handed down by tradition, but to be dreamed by each narrator. The shaman receives his power by dreaming ritualistic myths, which reveal to him his practices. The lengthy series of songs which are the essence of all ceremonies, and the mythical narratives connected with them, are also learned in dreams. It is probably a result of this importance of the dream-world and of the identification of myth and ceremony, of religious belief and religious practice, that ritualism is so slightly developed among the Mohave. Their geographical nearness and intercourse with the Hopi and other southwestern tribes, among whom ritualism and symbolism find perhaps their highest development on the continent north of Mexico, would certainly justify a contrary expectation. Both ceremonial actions and ceremonial paraphernalia and dress are developed only to a very slight extent. There is no initiation or society. The singing ceremonies, which with the exception of a few minor observances such as that for a girl's puberty, constitute all the Mohave ceremonies other than mourning ceremonies, are quite numerous, more than twenty being known. Some of these ceremonies are acknowledged to have been borrowed from other Yuman tribes, especially the Yuma, and these Indians no doubt have also acquired Mohave ceremonies. Some of the ceremonies are primarily mythical in character, others somewhat shamanistic. All are also sung in mourning. In addition there is a distinctive mourning ceremony held annually for important men.

BIBLIOGRAPHY.

Much of the material on which the statements in the preceding essay are based is information collected by the University of California's Ethnological and Archaeological Survey of California since 1901 and as yet unpublished. Of old accounts dealing with the religion of the Indians of California, the best is by the Franciscan missionary Boscana, entitled Chinigchinich and published in the 1846 edition of a volume by A. Robinson called Life in California. It deals with the Shoshonean Indians of Mission San Juan Capistrano. An occasional reference of value may be found in other works, such as Venegas' History of California. The series of translations and republications of early explorers in California and the Southwest, published in the Land of Sunshine, later Out West, beginning in 1899, is also convenient, though naturally it deals but incidentally with religion. Reid's account of the Indians of Los Angeles county, published in an early Los Angeles newspaper and republished by Alexander Taylor in the fourteenth volume of California Farmer in 1861, is particularly good, though less so on the side of religion than on most others. Stephen Powers' Tribes of California, issued in 1877 as the third volume of the Contributions to North American Ethnology, a government series, deals with the Indians of the greater part of the state and contains many references to their religious life. Powers is however often very inexact, and the value of his work is in its comprehensiveness rather than in its reliability. An important work is Creation Myths of Primitive America, by Jeremiah Curtin, which consists of a collection of myths from the Wintun and Yana of Northern California. The differences of form which these myths show from most Indian myths that have been published in translation are apparently chiefly due to the method of their presentation by the author. Curtin's introduction is very suggestive but exaggerated. Professor R. B. Dixon has brought out a paper on Maidu Myths, and another, a great part of which is devoted to religion, on the Northern Maidu, both in the seventeenth volume of the Bulletin of the American Museum of Natural History. These two contributions are among the most careful studies as yet made by a trained observer in any part of the state. The same author has also published briefer articles on Some Coyote Stories from the Maidu Indians of California, System and Sequence in Maidu Mythology, and Some Shamans of Northern California, in recent volumes of the Journal of American Folk-Lore, and on The Mythology of the Shasta-Achomawi in the American Anthropologist for 1905. Professor P. E. Goddard has published Life and Culture of the Hupa, the last portion of which refers to religion; and Hupa Texts (with both interlinear and current translations), almost all of which are religious in character. These two papers constitute Volume I of the University of California Publications in American Archaeology and Ethnology. In the Journal of American Folk-Lore for 1906 is a paper by the same author on Lassik Tales. Miss Constance Goddard DuBois has published a number of valuable papers on the Mission Indians, mainly concerning the mythology of the Diegueño, in the volumes of the Journal of American Folk-Lore for 1901, 1904, and 1906. In the American Anthropologist for 1905 Miss DuBois has an article on the Religious Ceremonies and Myths of the Mission Indians, while another paper on The Mythology of the Diegueños appears in the Proceedings of the Thirteenth International Congress of Americanists. From the present author there have appeared, in the second and fourth volumes of the series of American Archaeology and Ethnology, of the University of California Publications, Types of Indian Culture in California, in part treating of religion, and Indian Myths from South-Central California; in the Journal of American Folk-Lore between 1904 and 1906, A Ghost Dance in California, Wishosk Myths, and Two Myths of the Mission Indians; in the American Anthropologist for 1902, A Preliminary Sketch of the Mohave Indians. In the American Anthropologist for 1905 and 1906 the late Major H. N. Rust has two brief articles on The Obsidian Blades of California and A Puberty Ceremony of the Mission Indians. The Journal of American Folk-Lore has contained a rather confused article on The Cosmogony and Theogony of the Mojave Indians, by Capt. J. G. Bourke, in 1889, and others by G. W. James, on myths of the Mission Indians of Southern California, in 1902 and 1903. In the same Journal appeared in 1902 An Indian Myth from the

CPSIA information can be obtained at www.ICGtesting.com
Printed in the USA
LVOW06s1318230114

370690LV00001B/32/A